Walking Off Weight

The Workbook

THE 14-DAY, 14-STEP PROGRAM FOR LASTING WEIGHT LOSS

SAFE • SENSIBLE • SIMPLE • SATISFYING

ROBERT SWEETGALL, BS
Walking Consultant

ROBA WHITELEY, MS, RD
Nutritionist

ROBERT NEEVES, PhD
Physiologist

Published by:
Creative Walking, Inc.
P.O. Box 50296
Clayton, MO 63105

Copyright © 1989
Robert Sweetgall
Roba Whiteley
Robert Neeves
ISBN 0-939041-10-3

Books by the authors:
☐ **Fitness Walking** (Sweetgall/Rippe & Katch)
☐ **The Walking Wellness Teacher's Guide** (Sweetgall/Neeves)
☐ **The Walking Wellness Student Workbook** (Sweetgall/Neeves)
☐ **Walking for Little Children** (Sweetgall/Neeves)
☐ **The Walker's Journal** (Sweetgall/Dignam)
☐ **Treadmill Walking** (Sweetgall/Neeves)
☐ **Road Scholars** (Peleg/Sweetgall)

Book Credits:
☐ Cover Design: Cindy Paige
☐ Typesetting and Layout: Cheryl Adams
☐ Art and Graphics Consultation: Scott Bowman and Lynne Tesch
☐ Back Cover Photography: W.L. Gore & Associates (Fabrics Division),
Robert Craig and Eric Crossan

Table of Contents

In a world of diet quackery, authors throw out promises like fisherman cast lures. And you, the diet-conditioned reader, stand as prey to the thousands of cleverly worded diets of the decade.

Right this minute some 20 million Americans are swallowing the bait, buying into the ridiculous promises made on the front covers of two billion diet books printed annually. *"Lose 10 pounds the first 10 days."* And garbage like that. For $10 or less, you can buy hundreds of weight-loss fairy tales at your local bookstore. Wait a while, and these diet books can be yours for a buck.

When a fish bites a lure, it loses its life. When we bite at a phony diet, we lose money, pride and muscle mass. We're supposed to be smarter than fish. Yet a higher percentage of Americans fail at dieting than fish get caught at sea.

So before reading this book, realize that it comes without any sensational advertising claims. The only promise we make is to tell you the truth — the facts about fat — how you get it, how you lose it. The next 92 pages are built on 14 ideas — 14 steps for lighter living. Practice these steps and your body will become firmer, fitter and healthier.

You need not go on a crazy rampage in **Walking Off Weight**. All it takes is one little lifestyle change each day. A few extra steps, a little less fat. That's all. That's our promise!

The Authors

Rob Sweetgall *is a former DuPont Chemical Engineer who, in 1981, decided to leave the corporate ranks and his $50,000 job to walk across America. Since then, he has walked 11,208 miles of U.S. highways through 50 states in one year. He has presented seminars and workshops to over 250,000 people and authored or co-authored eight books on walking. The **Walking Wellness** curriculum he developed is used by thousands of schools nationally. To quote **The Wall Street Journal,** "When Sweetgall Walks, People Listen."*

Roba Whiteley MS,RD *received her Masters in Nutrition Science and has worked in behavioral weight control programs at The University of Pennsylvania and in her own private practice for 17 years. She has taught at Drexel University and the University of Delaware, presented seminars at hospitals and corporations, and hosted her own **Nutrition-Talk** radio show. Today, Roba presents **Walking Off Weight** seminars nationally, and does her walking along Florida's Gulf Coast beaches.*

Robert Neeves, PhD *is Co-Director of the University of Delaware Sports Science Laboratory and Professor of Exercise Physiology. Since receiving his PhD (University of Utah), he has served as a consultant to the U.S. Olympic Ice Skating, Ski, Luge and Bobsled Teams and co-authored four books on walking. Dr. Neeves is the former world record holder in the 50-meter Mens Breaststroke (Masters). Today, at the University of Delaware, Dr. Neeves teaches Exercise Physiology and Cardiac Rehabilitation, and conducts research in a variety of sports science areas.*

CHAPTER ONE

What Have You Got to Lose?

In your lifetime, you've probably gained and lost over 2000 pounds of body weight. That's a ton! Most likely you've tried numerous diets: fasting diets, nutri-this, nutri-that, high-protein shakes and diets named after doctors, cities, foods and movie stars.

If just one of those diets had worked for you, maybe you wouldn't be reading this book right now. But you are — which means you're willing to give *it* another shot.

Incidentally, you're not alone. About 20 million Americans are now dieting. Almost half of all U.S. adult middle-aged women are always dieting. Strange as it may seem, these numbers have remained fairly constant over the years — which tells you a lot about diet success rates.

The problem with diets is that they are temporary solutions (at best) to a permanent problem. The problem centers around metabolism — specifically low metabolism. The **less** you eat, the **lower** your metabolism goes. The **less** you move, the **lower** your metabolism goes. The **more** muscle you lose, the **lower** your metabolism goes. The **older** you get — yes, you guessed it — the **lower** your metabolism goes.

Most quick-fix diets are cleverly designed to rapidly dehydrate the body to produce the desired reading on the bathroom scale. Such rapid weight loss is primarily water loss along with some muscle-tissue loss. After the diet ends, and you return to normal eating habits (despite the behavior modification promises), you re-hydrate and regain weight. Unfortunately, you also gain back more fat than muscle. As a result, your new re-composed body is now fatter than it was before your last diet cycle. Your metabolism gets slower and slower after each succeeding diet. **Bottom line** — it becomes more difficult to burn off fat the next time around.

This is why so many dieters are digging their own graves. In a society where elevators, electric golf carts and push-button windows are becoming the norm, we and the *Nintendo Generation* are not burning enough calories.

As a nation we eat 10% less than our ancestors did in the 19th Century — yet we weigh 5% more. Wonder why? Back then, most of our Gross National Product was produced by manual labor. Now even the farmers are driving air-conditioned tractors with power-steering and push-button seats.

Consider Yankee Stadium. Built in the early 1920's, Babe Ruth's house seated 67,000 at capacity. When renovated in 1976, the stadium seated 57,000. *Reason:* The seats had to be made four inches wider to accommodate the average rump of the 1970's.

To counteract the sedentary lifestyle of the 80's, many younger folks have found it fashionable to plug in their 30-minute Fonda tapes. Others jog around the neighborhood. But how many senior citizens do you see pounding the pavement? However, millions of seniors are out walking.

This brings us to the subject of this book — a safe program of weight loss based on *sensible walking* and *satisfying nutrition*. Nothing fancy. Just good wholesome living. We're not asking you to run a marathon or dine on alfalfa grass.

The Walking Off Weight Program you are about to start is a systematic, 14-step plan for feeling good. About one-third of the steps deals with nutritional habits. Another third focuses on attitudes and the mind. The last third is concerned with movement — walking. As you'll soon discover, **Walking Off Weight** balances the *Three M's of Weight Loss: Mind, Mouth and Muscles*.

Walking Off Weight is based on making small daily improvements in your lifestyle. It's the additive effect of making a lot of small changes over the years that will guarantee long-lasting weight control.

For example, **Walking Off Weight** is a man gradually cutting back the size of his midnight ice-cream binges. It's a schoolteacher patrolling the schoolyard at recess on foot instead of with binoculars. **Walking Off Weight** is discovering that it takes one football field of walking to burn up one Plain M&M.

Right now, walk over to your full-length mirror and take a look at yourself. If you care to undress in your own privacy, do so. This mirror test takes only a few seconds and some guts. As you stand there facing yourself, try to picture the billions of fat cells that lie under your flesh. Now, picture them shrinking day by day — as you start making tiny changes in your eating and exercise walking habits.

Finally, take one last look in the mirror and ask yourself, *"What have I got to lose?"*

❖   ❖   ❖

CHAPTER TWO

A Systematic Approach to Walking Off Weight

Walking Off Weight is a **14-step** program designed for a **lifetime**. Its goals are to: (1) increase your understanding of nutrition, weight loss and walking, (2) decrease your body fat composition, (3) improve your aerobic capacity and overall health and (4) help you make lasting changes in your lifestyle.

Success comes by mastering the **14 steps**. This may seem easy — but hardly anyone masters all 14 on his or her first attempt. Conquer just half of these steps in your freshman year of *Walking Off Weight*, and you've done exceptionally well. The whole idea of this program is to develop healthy habits over a lifetime.

The 14-Step Program

Look to the right. You're staring at *The Big 14* — the 14 steps that will ultimately determine your long-term success in weight control. Some of these steps may not make complete sense to you now. But you will understand them as you read further.

In *Walking Off Weight*, your goal will be to focus on each of these steps **one day at a time**. One step . . . one day. This doesn't mean you'll need to master one step in only one day. Some steps may take you months of reinforcement. All we ask is that you start practicing these 14 concepts one at a time in the first 14 days of *Walking Off Weight*. **Practice** means **practice**, as in **doing** — getting outdoors to physically participate in the specific exercises recommended in the 84-page *Walking Off Weight Program* (Chapter 3). By doing these exercises (instead of just reading through them), you will become a believer. This is a lot more powerful and lasting than ordinary textbook learning.

The 14 Steps to Walking Off Weight

1. Diets Don't Work
2. The Three M's of Weight Loss
3. Picture Food as Fuel
4. Go for High-Octane Fuels
5. Eat Early
6. Think Oxygen
7. Walk After Meals
8. Walk for Time, Not Speed
9. Be A Swinger
10. The Magic Walking Formula
11. Walk Eight Days a Week
12. M&M's Are Really Football Fields
13. Little Changes Make Big Differences
14. Take the "P-Test"

The 14-Day Sequence for 14 Steps

On **Day #1** of **Walking Off Weight**, you start out by convincing yourself that diets are not the answer to long-lasting weight loss. The real answer you'll discover on **Day #2** has to do with *The Three M's: Mind, Mouth and Muscle*.

On **Day #3**, you'll begin to understand **Food as Fuel** and realize the difference between *appetite* and *hunger*. **Day #4** is dedicated to *High-Octane Fuels* and learning the importance of increasing your intake of complex carbohydrates and decreasing your consumption of fats.

On **Day #5,** the emphasis is on *breakfast* and *avoiding late-night snacking*. **Day #6** is dedicated to appreciating that *breathing more oxygen* means *burning more fat*.

On **Day #7**, you'll get to do a *mini-walk* after each meal, and on **Day #8**, you'll find that you **don't** have to walk super-fast to burn off the fat.

On **Day #9**, you'll learn the best way to *swing your arms* in a walking-weight loss program. On **Day #10**, you'll receive the ideal *Walking Prescription* — not only for weight loss, but for long-term health.

On **Day #11**, you'll see that it takes *more than walking three days a week* to be successful in a weight loss program. On **Day #12**, you'll discover that it takes *one football field* of walking (end zones included) to burn off *one Plain M&M Candy*.

On **Day #13**, you'll be pleasantly surprised to learn that the *little changes* in your lifestyle make the *big difference* in your waistline. And finally, on **Day #14,** you'll appreciate the value that *persistence* plays in lifelong weight management.

Why Take 14 Full Days to Practice 14 Simple Steps?

Many people think they can learn the **14-steps** in **one** day by reading ***Walking Off Weight*** on a quiet Sunday. As far as reading this book — yes — you could cover the 14 days of Chapter #3 in one day. If you're a fast reader, you could probably read this entire book in two hours.

There's only one problem. Habits don't change by reading *how* to do something. Change comes from **doing.** And that takes time. How much? We use one day per step, although it wouldn't hurt to spend several days on each of the 14 points. To keep things moving and exciting, we present you with **one challenge** for **one day** for **14 consecutive days**.

Each day focuses on a **specific objective** and **plan**. To help you achieve these **objectives**, 14 different sub-chapters are outlined in the 84 pages ahead. Each sub-chapter contains six pages complete with: (1) a review of the previous day's activity, (2) a summary of the new concept, (3) supporting thoughts and objectives, (4) an action planning exercise, (5) creative suggestions and (6) a personal diary page to document your progress. This six-page format is illustrated below.

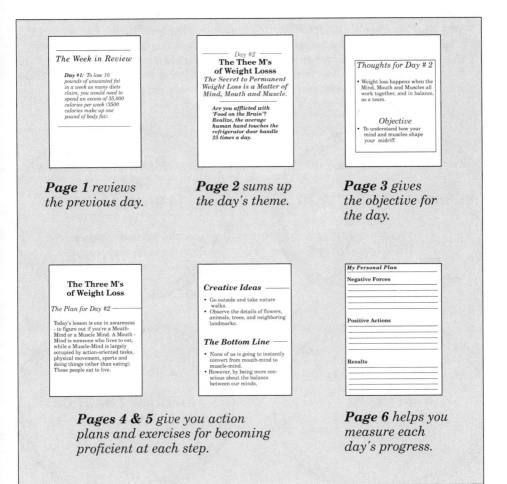

Page 1 *reviews the previous day.*

Page 2 *sums up the day's theme.*

Page 3 *gives the objective for the day.*

Pages 4 & 5 *give you action plans and exercises for becoming proficient at each step.*

Page 6 *helps you measure each day's progress.*

After the Fourteenth Day

After practicing **Walking Off Weight** for 14 days, you face your most important challenge — putting these steps into practice for the rest of your life. That's why **Walking Off Weight** never fades out of your life. You have an entire lifetime to perfect it. And you need an entire lifetime, because just when you think you've conquered one step — *zing* — a distraction enters into your life and — *zap* — your walking nutrition plan takes a temporary dive. That's okay. You're human. You're allowed some occasional slippages. As long as you're aware of them, you can collect yourself and get back on track.

The Long Haul is what really counts. In fact, as you'll soon read, short-term crash weight loss can actually hurt your long-term weight management. So if you're in this game to drop a few quick pounds, maybe you ought to drop this book. There are plenty of $2.95 paperbacks which can help your body flush out five pounds of pure water this week.

But if you want to take the safe and sensible approach, just follow the **14** common sense steps of nutrition and walking exercise which lie ahead.

In summary, this entire **Walking Off Weight Program** is best implemented in four distinct phases. **Phase One:** Take that hard look in the mirror and say, "*Yes, it's time for a change.*" **Phase Two:** Begin to read, learn and practice the 14-day, 14-step **Walking Off Weight** exercises. **Phase Three:** On your 14th day, take a brief quiz to discover your **new** strengths and **old** weaknesses. **Phase Four:** Take a deep breath, relax and have fun playing for the rest of your thin and beautiful life, without having to worry about spending a fortune on any more weight-loss concoctions.

The best of health and walking to you — forever.

PHASE ONE

PERSONAL COMMITMENT

I'm ready to start my Walking Off Weight Program!

PHASE TWO

14 DAYS, 14 STEPS

I'll play one exercise game a day for the next 14 days.

PHASE THREE

SELF-QUIZ

How am I doing?

PHASE FOUR

LIFETIME PRACTICE

I'm getting better with age!

CHAPTER THREE

The Walking Off Weight Program

I n the next 14 days you will have an opportunity to take 14 steps for improved weight control. The steps are simple and painless. You take them one day at a time: 14 steps in 14 days. Each day you'll be challenged to participate in a new creative *Walking Off Weight* exercise. By physically doing these exercises (most of them take 30 minutes or less), you will learn the safest and most sensible ways to burn off excess body fat.

On the 14th day, as you complete your first pass through *Walking Off Weight*, you'll discover an *Evaluation Scorecard* to help you take inventory of your habits (page 90). Regardless of your *Evaluation Scores*, be *grateful* for the health you have — and be *patient* for the body changes which will happen as you keep practicing these 14 basic steps through life.

Also, be happy! The best is yet to come.

❖   ❖   ❖

A Word of Caution: Readers of **Walking Off Weight** *should understand that there is inherent risk in all types of exertional activities, whether it's physical labor at home or even low-intensity, weight-loss walking. Furthermore, this risk increases as we age and as certain lifestyle "risk factors," such as high blood pressure, cholesterol, sedentary living, obesity, smoking and family history, begin to develop in our lives. If you are over 35 years, have any of these "risk factors" present in your life — or if you suspect their presence or have a family history of heart disease, it is recommended that you see your doctor, have a physical examination, and discuss the specific nature of the* **walking-weight loss program** *you are about to undertake.*

It is also recommended that you coordinate your **walking-weight loss program** *with a registered dietitian to insure that all of your nutritional needs are being satisfied.*

In many cases it is advisable to have a medically supervised treadmill tolerance test to determine your safe exertional levels. Jim Fixx was advised to take such a test, but he declined to do so. And like many who suffer heart attacks, he never got a second chance.

The Week in Review

*Before beginning each of your next 14 **Walking Off Weight** practice days, take a moment to reinforce your learning by reading **The Week in Review**. These review pages will improve your understanding of **walking** and **weight loss** and support you in your lifestyle changes.*

Diets Don't Work

The Real Reason Diets Don't Work, and How to Free Yourself from Diet Quackery

The majority of people who diet gain back most of their lost weight within one year of going off their diets. Many end up regaining more than they had lost, creating even bigger problems. Regardless of their claims, diets are only a temporary solution to a permanent problem.

Quick-fix diets are dangerous because they lead to rapid weight loss, much of which is muscle loss. When you lose muscle, you lose the best fat-burning tissue in your body. The net result — your metabolism slows down.

After you go off a diet and return to normal eating patterns and lifestyle, your body no longer burns fuel at your pre-diet rate because your muscle mass is lower. Consequently, you regain weight even faster. Plus, it becomes more difficult to burn off the fat the next time around. And so the cycle continues; quick-fix diet → muscle loss → lower metabolism → regain weight as fat → restart new diet → lose more muscle → and so on.

The faster you free your mind from quick-fix, weight-loss diets, the sooner you'll be able to focus on the real solution: **moving your large muscles to increase your metabolism and burn fat.**

For starters, try to erase the word **diet** from your vocabulary. How? Take your family of fat cells out on a diet-detoxification walk!

Thoughts for Day #1

- If diet book publishers were required to give refunds to all of their disappointed readers, would a publisher ever have the guts to print another diet book?

- If just one diet in the history of the world really worked, would it be necessary for new diet books to be written year after year?

- The average American attempts to use some form of dieting twice a year. That's over 400 million diet attempts annually.

- Every time you diet and lose fat-burning muscle tissue, you become less and less able to burn fat and control your weight.

Objectives

- To realize that diets are not the answer to permanent weight loss.

- To begin a new life completely free of fad-diet programs.

Diets Don't Work

The Plan for Day #1

Diet Detoxification. How many diets have you tried in your lifetime? Can you remember even half of them? Are they even worth remembering?

Today on **Day #1** of your **Walking Off Weight** program, your goal is to start a **Diet-Detoxification** process to *completely free yourself of future tendencies to diet.* To achieve this, start out by taking a short walk for about 15 to 20 minutes or whatever distance feels comfortable to you. Take along a pen and four small index cards labeled as follows.

Diets that have failed:

Diets Don't Work Because:

My Current Feelings on this Walk:

My New Pledge:

"I promise not to go on any new or old diets for one year in order to give my new walking program a fair chance."

Name   Date   Witness

Your objective on the *Diet-Detoxification Walk* is to: (1) recall diets that have failed in your life and why they didn't work and (2) think about walking as a pleasant alternative to dieting. Record your thoughts on your index cards immediately after ending your walk. At that time, see if you're willing to sign your pledge card. If you are, commemorate today as your *Declaration of Independence from Diets Day (DID Day).*

Companion Walking Exercise. Do this same *Diet-Detoxification Walk* with a companion. On your walk, exchange your most ridiculous diet stories. Then take a few moments to fill out your index cards, and witness each other's signatures.

Turning Day #1 into a Fun Party. Throw a *Diets-Don't-Work Party* for a small group of your friends. Have everyone show up in walking clothes with his or her most ridiculous diet book in hand. Begin the party with a walk, followed by toasts around a campfire (or fireplace). End the party by throwing your diet books into the fire and wishing each other well in your new **Walking Off Weight** programs.

Extra Credit. Mail us your funniest or most ridiculous diet story (or send us a photocopy of your four index cards). For sharing your stories, you'll receive a decorative **Walking Off Weight** patch for your favorite walking outfit.

*Mail stories to: Creative Walking, Inc., P.O. Box 50296, Clayton, MO 63105

Creative Ideas

- Continue your **Walking Off Weight** index card collection by keeping journal notes on observations you make on your *weight-loss walks*. Keep updating your index cards and you'll be amazed at their value and meaning to you in years to come.

- Whenever you hear about a new "exciting" diet, refer back to the four index cards you completed on Day #1.

- For reinforcement, picture yourself measuring food portions and living on powdered diet shakes for the rest of your life.

- Continue taking *Diet-Detoxification Walks* with various friends throughout the year, and see how many diets you can list.

The Bottom Line

*Once and for all, can you truly say you've "had it" with diets for the rest of your life? Are you ready to start a new life of sensible eating and pleasurable exercise? If so, you've taken the first great step in the **walk for lasting weight loss**.*

My Personal Plan for Day #1

NEGATIVE FORCES
(List any obstacles you must overcome to succeed on Day #1)

Example: My friend, Susan, always begs me to start a new diet with her.

_____

_____

_____

_____

_____

POSITIVE ACTIONS
(List the specific steps and plans you will take starting today)

Example: I'm going to take Susan out on a diet-detoxification walk and have her read Step 1 *of* **Walking Off Weight**.

_____

_____

_____

_____

_____

RESULTS
(List changes in your attitude, behavior or physical being due to your actions)

Example: Now, Susan and I walk regularly together without the temptation of trying fad diets.

_____

_____

_____

_____

_____

The Week in Review

Day #1: *To lose 10 pounds of unwanted fat in a week as many diets claim, you would need to spend an excess of* **35,000** *calories per week (3500 calories make up one pound of body fat). That would mean cutting back your food intake by* **5000** *calories per day* (**5000** calories/day x **7** days = **35,000** calories) — *or increasing your walking by only* **50** *miles per day* (**50** miles/day x **100** calories/mile walked x **7** days = **35,000** calories). *As you can plainly see, neither of these plans is reasonable, which leads us to one conclusion. . . . Anyone who loses 10 pounds the first week is losing mostly water and muscle — not fat!*

The Three M's of Weight Loss

The Secret to Permanent Weight Loss is a Matter of Mind, Mouth and Muscle.

Are you afflicted with "Food-on-the-Brain"? The average human hand touches the refrigerator door handle 26 times a day. That's a lot for three meals. What percentage of your waking hours are spent thinking about food? In contrast, how many hours a day do you think about moving your muscles?

To successfully manage your weight, there needs to be a balance among three characters that live within your body: *Meditative Mind, Mischievous Mouth and Mighty Muscle.*

Your **Mind** is the *judge* in the courtroom. It is constantly listening to voices from two parts of your body: your **Mouth** and your **Muscles**. Your **Mouth** pleads to walk towards the refrigerator. Your **Muscles** plead to walk in the other direction. A good *judge* (**Mind**) knows how to keep both parties in the courtroom (**Muscles** and **Mouth**) under control and in balance.

Thoughts for Day #2

- Weight loss happens when the **Mind**, **Mouth** and **Muscles** work together, and in balance, as a team.

- If your **Mind** is always worrying about your **Mouth**, your **Muscles** are going to get a complex and hide behind a column of fat.

- Most overweight Americans spend too much mental energy on *munching* and not enough physical energy *moving their muscles*.

- If we as a nation thought more about **movement** and less about **food**, we could lose one billion pounds. That's four pounds of U.S. fat per citizen — if each of us added just **eight minutes** a day of walking to our lifestyles.

Objective

- To understand how your **Mind**, **Mouth** and **Muscles** shape your **Midriff.**

The Three M's of Weight Loss

The Plan for Day #2

Today's goal is to figure out if you're a **Mouth-Mind** or a **Muscle-Mind**. A **Mouth-Mind** is someone who *lives to eat*, while a **Muscle-Mind** is largely occupied by action-oriented tasks, physical movement, sports and doing things (other than eating). These people *eat to live*.

Your exercise for Day #2 is to keep a **Mouth-Mind / Muscle-Mind** scorecard as shown below. Whenever your mind shifts to the subject of food or eating, put a check in the left hand column of a 3" x 5" index card. Whenever your mind switches over to thinking about any kind of physical movement (i.e. walking to the store or around your parking lot, or about playing golf or tennis, etc.), check the right hand column.

At the end of Day #2, tally your check marks and see if you're surprised. Then go out on a walk (either alone or with a friend) and brainstorm on how you could spend more time balancing your **Mouth-Mind** *and* **Muscle-Mind**.

MOUTH-MIND	MUSCLE-MIND
✓ ✓ ✓ ✓ ✓	✓ ✓ ✓
✓ ✓ ✓ ✓ ✓	
✓ ✓ ✓ ✓	

Suggestion: You will get a lot more out of this exercise if you keep your **Mouth-Mind / Muscle-Mind** cards close at hand during the day. For example, keep them accessible in a pocket, a desk drawer or a handbag so that you'll be able to add your check marks as soon as new thoughts occur in your mind.

Creative Ideas

If you're constantly plagued by *food-on-the-brain*, try the following:

- Go outside and take nature walks. Observe the details of flowers, trees, animals, and neighborhood landmarks.

- Keep trying to picture your **Mind** as the **Judge** in a courtroom, trying to be fair to both parties — your **Mouth** and your **Muscles**. As in paid political announcements, give equal time to both parties. In other words, try to counter each thought on food with an equal and opposite thought on physical movement.

- Play a game with a friend in which one of you plays **Mouth-Mind** (by constantly talking about food) and the other plays **Muscle-Mind** (by constantly talking about physical activity). Try to end the game by moving instead of eating.

- Instantly name five *mini movements* you could do right now. Then see how many of these you could quickly do in the next three minutes.

Mini Movements
• Stand up and stretch
• Water a plant
• Turn off one useless light in your house
• Walk outside and smell the night air
• Pick up a piece of paper on the floor

The Bottom Line

*None of us is going to instantly convert from a **Mouth-Mind** to **Muscle-Mind**. However, by being more conscious about the balance between our minds, muscles and mouths, we will begin to improve in the weight management game.*

My Personal Plan for Day #2

NEGATIVE FORCES
(List any obstacles you must overcome to succeed on Day #2)

_____

_____

_____

_____

_____

_____

POSITIVE ACTIONS
(List the specific steps and plans you will take starting today)

_____

_____

_____

_____

_____

_____

RESULTS
(List changes in your attitude, behavior or physical being due to your actions)

_____

_____

_____

_____

_____

_____

The Week in Review

Day #1: *When you lose a pound of muscle on a rapid weight-loss diet, you lose a pound of your best fat-burning tissue.*

Day #2: *One of the good things about walking out-of-doors is that it keeps your* **Mind** *and* **Mouth** *away from the refrigerator.*

Day #3

Picture Food as Fuel

Understanding the Difference Between Appetite and Hunger and Appreciating Food Simply as Fuel

Food is fuel. It is nothing more. It is not a reward, a temptation or an appeasement. Nor is it an anti-depressant. And it doesn't need to be the centerpiece of every family gathering. It is not something that needs to occupy the two-minute commercial break in a football game.

The quicker you come to value food as fuel, the sooner you will be in control of your waistline. Success hinges on understanding the difference between *appetite* and *hunger*.

Appetite is in your head. It's a suggestive sensation in your brain which leads you to the refrigerator. *Hunger* is in your stomach. It's a physical need crying out, sending signals to your brain, telling you it's time to re-fuel. If you learn to re-fuel on your *hunger* cues, your energy will increase and you're body fat will decrease.

Thoughts for Day #3

- *Hunger* is physical; *appetite* is mental. When it comes to food, behave like animals. They eat instinctively when hunger strikes. By the way, how many fat animals do you see in the jungle?

- Hunger is your friend. It lets you know when your body needs fuel. The best time to eat is when you're just starting to get hungry. If you wait too long, excessive hunger may drive you to overeat.

- When you see a slice of strawberry cheesecake, your **Mouth** starts telling you, *"You're getting hungry."* In reality, *"You're getting an appetite."*

- If we treated our cars the way we treat our bodies, there would be *log jams* at every gas pump in America. Fortunately, most of us pull up to the gas pump only when our tanks are near empty — not 15 times a day.

Objective

- To learn to appreciate *food as fuel* — not as a social ritual, reward, anti-depressant or something to fill space and time.

Picture Food as Fuel

The Plan for Day #3

The *Why?* Game: Today you're going to get to play **The *Why?* Game** — as in *"Why are you eating this?"* Here's how the game works. Every time you eat something today—anything—simply check the **Appetite (A)** or the **Hunger (H)** boxes next to the word or phrase describing *why* you ate.

APPETITE - HUNGER SCORECARD   *[A = Appetite   H = Hunger]*

A ☐☐☐ Depression	A ☐☐☐ Right Time of Day	H ☐ Hunger
A ☐☐☐ Reward Time	A ☐☐☐ Nothing Better To Do	H ☐ Hunger
A ☐☐☐ Frustration	A ☐☐☐ Taste Temptation	H ☐ Hunger
A ☐☐☐ It Was There	A ☐☐☐ Social Pressure	H ☐ Hunger
A ☐☐☐ Showing Love	A ☐☐☐ Stress Reduction	H ☐ Hunger
A ☐☐☐ To Keep Busy	A ☐☐☐ Mandated by Diet-Plan	H ☐ Hunger
A ☐☐☐ Free Food	A ☐☐☐ Unconscious Move	H ☐ Hunger
A ☐☐☐ Out of Habit	A ☐☐☐ No Reason at All	H ☐ Hunger
A ☐☐☐ Super Craving	A ☐☐☐ Just Flew in my Mouth	H ☐ Hunger

---

*Example: If you ate due to **hunger**, check one of the **(H)** boxes. If you ate for any reason other than **hunger**, check an **appetite** box next to the phrase which best describes the real driving force behind your eating at that moment.*

On Day #3, take a few minutes at bedtime to review your **Appetite - Hunger Scorecard**. For all the times you checked **appetite**, ask yourself *"What could I have done instead of eating at that particular moment?"* Then, try playing this game tomorrow with the three new rules shown below.

LIVE TOMORROW THIS WAY

Rule 1   If you're **hungry**, eat slowly until the hunger disappears.
Rule 2   If your **appetite** is up, walk until you feel the sensation of hunger. Then follow **Rule 1**.
Rule 3   If you're **not hungry** or if your **appetite** is not strong, do anything other than eat. If **hunger** comes, follow **Rule 1**. If **appetite** surfaces, follow **Rule 2**.

---

*Take time to chew your food. It takes about 20 minutes from the time you chew your food until it's into your body to tell your brain to shut off the hunger alarm. If you eat too fast, you'll eat more than you need to take care of hunger, thereby overfilling your gas tank.

Creative Ideas

If you find appetite dominating your life, for example if you suffer from *food-on-the-brain* — consider the following suggestions:

- Substitute other activities into your daily life that get your *mind* and *body* away from food.

- Step outside and walk around the neighborhood just to get away from the kitchen scenery and food.

- Use as many of your senses as possible when eating: taste, smell, touch. Feel the texture of food — for example, the chewy, gutsy flavor in whole grain or the crunch of veggies. Savor each bite.

Follow Up

Keep practicing **Rule 1**, **Rule 2** and **Rule 3** of **The *Why?* Game** until more of your eating happens because of **hunger** instead of **appetite**.

The Bottom Line

Food is fuel. It gives you energy to drive your body through the day. If you start thinking of food in this light, your eating habits and weight-loss plan will improve dramatically.

My Personal Plan for Day #3

NEGATIVE FORCES
(List any obstacles you must overcome to succeed on Day #3)

_____

_____

_____

_____

_____

_____

POSITIVE ACTIONS
(List the specific steps and plans you will take starting today)

_____

_____

_____

_____

_____

RESULTS
(List changes in your attitude, behavior or physical being due to your actions)

_____

_____

_____

_____

_____

_____

The Week in Review

Day #1: *Why do you think that so many diets are designed with magic powders, shakes and various nutritional supplements, typically costing $25 to $50 a week?*

Day #2: *If you truly start to picture food as fuel, you'll begin to view the* **mouth** *as the orifice through which food passes to re-fuel the* **muscles**. *Then, your* **mind** *can serve as the decision-maker for selecting the best fuels to buy. That's teamwork.*

Day #3: Hunger *is your friend. It lets you know when your body needs fuel.* **Appetite** *is an imposter who knocks on your door long before* **hunger** *has a chance to arrive. If you stay busy, away from the temptations of food, the imposter,* **appetite**, *will feel ignored and walk away from your unanswered door.*

Day #4

Go for High-Octane Fuels

Learning to Replace Fat with Complex Carbohydrates

Fatty foods are fattening. Take butter. One tablespoon contains 100 calories. One tablespoon of pure sugar (100% carbohydrate) is only 46 calories. When you swallow fat, you're taking in nine calories per gram. Carbohydrates and proteins contain only four calories per gram. Furthermore, when you eat 100 calories of carbohydrate, the body spends approximately 27% of those calories just to process the carbohydrates internally. Eat 100 calories of fat and only 3% of those calories will be spent on internal processing. That's a 24% difference! That's why *"Not all calories are created equal."*

Besides the calorie issue, carbohydrates are healthier than fats for your cardiovascular system — especially your blood vessels. High fat intake is associated with elevated blood cholesterol levels, hardening of the arteries and various forms of cancer.

In summary, carbohydrates are your best *high-octane* fuel. They're *less expensive* to buy and *better* for the *life of your heart and blood vessels* — and they're far less fattening. So for reasons of finance, fitness and fat reduction, it pays to replace seductive tasting fats with energizing carbohydrates.

Thoughts for Day #4

- If the best fuel at the gas pump was also the least expensive, wouldn't you buy the best?

- Complex carbohydrates are the best and least expensive fuels for the human internal combustion engine.

- Carbohydrate-rich foods like leafy salads and baked potatoes are not fattening — until we drip fatty dressings and sour cream all over them.

Objectives

- To gradually **increase** the ratio of *complex carbohydrates* to *fats* in your daily fuel supply.

Go for High-Octane Fuels

The Plan for Day #4

Cutting the Fat: In the 1980's, the popular wisdom has been to *cut fat intake to 30% or less of your total calories.* In the 1970's, the target was 35%.

But who on earth calculates calories to know what 30% or 35% fat calories are in terms of real food. You'd need to keep and analyze detailed food logs the rest of your life to know your percentage of fat intake. One thing we do know, Americans eat too much fat. Estimates for adults indicate that over 35% of their calories come from fat. For kids it's over 40%! That's not healthy.*

So today, on **Day #4** of your **Walking Off Weight** program, let's focus on *cutting excess dietary fat* by making little changes in your eating habits. Start off Day #4 by making a series of small (yet lasting) dietary changes to *reduce your total fat intake* and *increase your total carbohydrate intake.* To accomplish this, cut back or eliminate completely one food from *Group A* every day. Likewise, eat more of the kinds of foods shown in *Group B.* This will shift your fuel supply towards high-octane carbohydrates.

Group A — Fat

Reduce your intake of these items day by day. All Hard Cheeses, Cheesecake, Anything Fried, Red Meat, Cakes & Chocolates, Butter & Margarine, Nuts & Peanut Butter, Bacon, Sausage, Ice-Cream, Whole Milk, Most Whole Milk Products, Salad Dressings and Most Fast-Food Fare.

Group B — Complex Carbohydrates

Increase your intake of these items day by day. Pears, Bananas, Apples, Oranges, Oat Bran Muffins, Bread, Pancakes, Pasta, Potatoes, Green Beans, Corn, Soups, Carrots, Tomatoes, Green Leafy Vegetables, Low-fat or Non-fat Dairy Foods (milk, yogurt, etc.).

So where do you begin today? Start by promising yourself, *"I'll cut back one fatty food (like my afternoon Snickers) from my diet — just one."* Similarly, make one firm commitment to add one carbohydrate-rich food (like an apple) to your diet — just one. Record your changes and substitutions on **Your Fat-Carbohydrate Scoreboard**. For a long-term goal, keep building your lists over this entire year.

*Based on research such as the Framingham Heart Study, we now know that there is a strong correlation between fat in the diet, being overweight and heart disease.

My Dietary Fat Reductions ✍

_____

_____

_____

_____

_____

_____

My Carbohydrate Additions ✍

_____

_____

_____

_____

_____

_____

Example 1: Assume your average daily food intake is 2000 calories of which 40% is fat (800 calories). As part of your Day #4 Action Plan, you've decided to stop buttering your morning pancakes and substitute a few teaspoons of strawberry jam. The butter and jam portions each contain about 80 calories, except the butter is 100% fat and the jam is 100% carbohydrate. **Question**: What impact would this simple substitution have on your percent fat intake?

Before (80 calories of butter on pancakes)	800 Calories of Fat per day	→	$\dfrac{800}{2000}$ = 40% fat
After (80 calories of jam on pancakes)	720 Calories of Fat per day	→	$\dfrac{720}{2000}$ = 36% fat

Footnote: Would you really miss the layer of melted butter swimming under a pool of maple syrup? Maybe at first, but after a while, you may enjoy the taste of various fruit preserves even more.

Example 2: What's more fattening: 500 calories of spaghetti marinara or 500 calories of cheesecake? ***Answer:*** 500 calories of cheesecake. ***Reason:*** It takes approximately 135 calories of internal body energy to process the *pasta* meal by chewing, digesting and breaking down the carbohydrates for storage and use. The remaining 365 calories — if not used — eventually will get stored as fat. The *cheesecake* requires about 25 calories of internal body energy for processing. In effect, you receive a 110 calorie rebate for eating the carbohydrate-rich spaghetti instead of the high-fat cheesecake.

The Bottom Line

All calories are not equal! By lowering your fatty food intake, you'll be doing both your waistline and your heart a favor. The easiest way to begin is to attack one fatty food on your daily menu at a time. In its place, just add your favorite carbohydrate-rich food containing approximately the same number of calories.

My Personal Plan for Day #4

NEGATIVE FORCES
(List any obstacles you must overcome to succeed on Day #4)

_____

_____

_____

_____

_____

POSITIVE ACTIONS
(List the specific steps and plans you will take starting today)

_____

_____

_____

_____

_____

RESULTS
(List changes in attitude, behavior or physical being due to your actions)

_____

_____

_____

_____

_____

The Week in Review

Day #1: *The faster you lose weight on a crash diet, the greater the tendency to lose muscle mass, making it nearly impossible for you to keep off the weight you lost. A sensible weight-loss rate is one pound (of fat) per week.*

Day #2: *One way to keep **The Mouth** in check, is to make sure both **The Muscle** and **The Mind** are present in the "courtroom" to participate in the decision-making process.*

Day #3: *There is nothing wrong with re-fueling your body six or more times a day in small feedings. In fact, this is more advantageous than gorging yourself once or twice a day.*

Day #4: *High-octane fuels (carbohydrates) take up more space than fat — both on your plate and in your stomach. That's one reason why carbohydrates are generally more satisfying.*

Day #5

Eat Early

Switching from Late-Night Snacks to Early Morning Breakfasts

The 500 calories you eat in the morning are not as fattening as the 500 calories you eat late at night. Morning calories fuel you for the day; the late evening calories get stored in fat cells on your hips and thighs as you sleep.

Skipping breakfast, a common weight-loss technique, lowers your morning metabolism. Plus it sets you up for crash food binges later in the afternoon and evening.

Eating a substantial breakfast helps maintain proper blood sugar levels throughout the morning, minimizing irritability and lethargy. It also raises your morning metabolism, helping you burn extra calories — even while driving to work.

Food consumed right before bedtime serves no useful physiological purpose and winds up spending the night finding a home inside your fat cells.

The trick is to start off the day with a *full tank* of carbohydrate fuel (breakfast) — and end the day without *topping off your tank* at midnight.

Thoughts for Day #5

- Skipping breakfast slows down your morning metabolism. As a result, you burn less calories as your body conserves fuel while waiting for its next meal.

- Next time you scoop out 400 calories of ice-cream and butterfat before the 11 pm news, ask yourself how many calories it really takes to focus a pair of eyeballs on the TV.

- Breakfast calories provide energy all day long. Late night calories find a home in your fat cells while you sleep.

- End each day with just enough reserve fuel to carry you through the night. If you're not *hungry* in the morning — you probably ate too much, too late at night.

Objectives

- To consume more fuel earlier in the day.

- To avoid late-night *fill-ups*.

Eat Early

The Plan for Day #5

To get in the habit of eating more in the morning and less at night, we are going to play a game called **Food Curfew**. If you haven't eaten "it" by your assigned curfew hour, "it" gets deposited into a *curfew basket* or *doggy bag* and stored until morning when you actually need it.

The difficult question is:*What's a reasonable curfew time to assign in this game?* 7 p.m.? 8 p.m.? 9 p.m.? 10 p.m.? The answer depends on your daily schedule. When do you get home from work? When do you normally sit down to dinner? Could you live with a curfew set right after dinner?

Example: Lately, little 100-calorie peanut butter / cracker sandwiches have been winding up on paper party plates in your lap along with a cold glass of milk right around the time the 11 o'clock News comes on. Starting tonight, you're going to set an arbitrary eating curfew at 8 pm. The peanut butter and milk will wait until morning to supplement your skimpy toast-and-coffee breakfast. **Question:** *How will this eating modification shift your caloric distribution.*

BEFORE CURFEW		
Breakfast →	200	calories
Lunch →	600	calories
Dinner →	1000	calories
Snacks →	200	calories
Total =	2000	calories

% Calories by Mid-Day = 40%
% Late Night Calories = 10%

AFTER CURFEW		
Breakfast →	400	calories
Lunch →	600	calories
Dinner →	1000	calories
Snacks →	0	calories
Total =	2000	calories

% Calories by Mid-Day = 50%
% Late Night Calories = 0%

Changing Your Curfew: In this game you need to be both *firm* and *flexible*. *Firm* means when you set a curfew, you try to live by it. *Flexible* means you can re-set your curfew any time. Once you do, you honor it. If your curfew times keep getting earlier and earlier in the evening, that's a positive sign of self-improvement. Congratulations!

Creative Ideas

- At night, as you deposit food in your *curfew basket* or *doggy bag*, think how you'll enjoy that food in the morning for breakfast. If these leftovers are inappropriate for breakfast in the morning, freeze them for another meal — or just throw them out.

- Keep your *curfew basket* out of site and out of mind.

- Set a food curfew that's reasonable to live by.

- Whenever you're tempted to have a late night treat, picture where that snack will wind up as you sleep.

The Bottom Line

*Learning to **eat early** is one of the most difficult of the 14 **Walking Off Weight** steps to master. Yet, it is extremely important. But you don't have to tackle this habit all at once. You can start with an 11:30 p.m. curfew, and over a period of months work your way down to 11 p.m., 10 p.m., 9 p.m. and 8 p.m.. Eventually you'll be hooked on hearty breakfasts instead of late-night junk.*

My Personal Plan for Day #5

NEGATIVE FORCES
(List any obstacles you must overcome to succeed on Day #5)

_____

_____

_____

_____

_____

POSITIVE ACTIONS
(List the specific steps and plans you will take starting today)

_____

_____

_____

_____

_____

RESULTS
(List changes in your attitude, behavior or physical being due to your actions)

_____

_____

_____

_____

_____

The Week in Review

Day #1: *If you try one of today's popular low-carbohy-drate, high-protein diets, remember — you're depriving your body of the critical fuel it needs to function.*

Day #2: *If your body is a true democracy, then your* **mind, mouth** *and* **muscles** *should be discussing, compromising and planning throughout the day on how to run the "government." Dictators have big, over-bearing* **mouths** *and tunnelvision* **minds.**

Day #3: *Thinking of food as fuel, picture how far you could walk based on the caloric content of the following fuels: 1 apple, 1 slice pizza and 1 snip of celery.* ***Answers:*** *1 mile, 3 miles and 10 feet, respectively.*

Day #4: *The difference between eating an apple (rich in carbohydrates) and a chocolate candy bar (rich in fat) for an energy lift, is that the apple will raise and maintain your blood sugar levels and energy much longer than the chocolate bar. The chocolate bar also has considerably more calories and fat than the apple.*

Day #5: *Forget traditional breakfasts like bacon and eggs. Expand your breakfast menu to include many of the regular foods you eat during the normal course of a day.*

Day #6

Think Oxygen

The More Oxygen You Breathe, The More Fat You Burn

Oxygen is free! So don't be afraid to use it. The more total oxygen you can process in a day, the more body fat you'll burn up that day. This concept is basic to weight loss and fat reduction.

To visualize this point, picture millions of tiny cellular structures housed within our muscles. These structures act like *small furnaces*, burning oxygen, fat and sugar to make energy essential for body movements. As your activity levels increase, so does the oxygen demand in these *cellular furnaces*. As you become more active (i.e. rising off the couch) your oxygen demand begins to increase. Consequently, you start to breathe harder, enabling more oxygen to be delivered to your working muscles to burn more fat and carbohydrates.

In summary, the amount of oxygen you breathe at any given time is a fair representation of how much fuel your *furnaces* are burning at that time. The greater your oxygen consumption — the greater your caloric expenditure and fat burn.

The key, then, is focusing on using greater amounts of oxygen by elevating our breathing rates naturally throughout the day — even if just on short-duration tasks such as . . . mowing the lawn . . . walking the workplace hallways more briskly . . . striding across the parking lot . . . walking a few hills . . . or climbing a few extra stairs. Activities that increase your oxygen consumption also increase the burning of fat.

So Think Oxygen! And look for opportunities to breathe more of it!

Thoughts for Day #6

- The more **oxygen** you process — the more fat you burn. Every time you increase your breathing rate, you're helping yourself burn more fat and sugar to produce more energy for muscle movement.

- One minute of moderately elevated breathing — as in walking one city block — helps you burn five extra calories.

- Anytime you breathe heavier, due to physical exertion, your body burns extra fuel.

- Climbing a few flights of stairs for two minutes a day can help you burn 15 extra calories. That translates to a 1.5-pound fat loss after a year. All because you took a few extra steps, uphill, against gravity.

Objectives

- To appreciate that when we increase our breathing rate to perform physical tasks, we consume more oxygen and burn more fuel.

- To get in the habit of **being** more physical . . . **breathing** more oxygen . . . and **burning** more fat.

Think Oxygen

The Plan for Day #6

You are about to celebrate *National Oxygen Day (N.O.D.)*! This holiday is a tribute to *Ollie Oxygen*, a molecule of oxygen who gave up his life to kill a fat cell way back in the *Battle of the Bulge*. As a result of Ollie's bravery, millions of oxygen molecules have since been inspired to do the same — to consume and conquer fat. And right now *Ollie's Army of Oxygen Molecules* are ready to help you win your *War on Fat*. All you need to do is activate your "fat-burning warriors" on this special *N.O.D.* Memorial Holiday.

In celebration of *N.O.D. Day*, your goal is to pay tribute to *Ollie Oxygen* by significantly raising your breathing rate **ten (10)** times today alone! You can do this in any number of ways — climb a few extra flights of stairs...take a walking detour up a hill...or just pick up the pace on a routine errand down the hallway. Do anything with a little extra vigor to pick up your breathing rate — even if it's only for 30 seconds or a minute. Remember, 60 seconds of accelerated breathing due to extra physical exertion translates to at least five calories of extra fat burn!

Each time you bring yourself to an accelerated breathing rate, try to picture the "furnace analogy" of your muscles burning extra fat. Then make a brief entry on the chart below. See if you can participate in **10** special oxygen events today.

NATIONAL OXYGEN DAY

Your Oxygen Event (Describe your exertion)	Extra Calories Spent (Estimate at 5 cal/min)
1 _____	1 _____
2 _____	2 _____
3 _____	3 _____
4 _____	4 _____
5 _____	5 _____
6 _____	6 _____
7 _____	7 _____
8 _____	8 _____
9 _____	9 _____
10 _____	10 _____

Creative Ways to Use More Oxygen

- Resist using remote controls on the TV.

- Park as far away from your building entrance as possible.

- Add a detour on your mall shopping tour.

- Look for a set of stairs to climb every day.

- Walk on grass and gravel instead of smooth asphalt (30% to 50% increase in energy expenditure).

- Walk more on hilly ground.

- Walk backwards sometimes (25% increase in energy expenditure).

- Avoid sitting for more than 15 consecutive minutes.

- Add one-minute intervals of brisk walking on your walks.

- Swing your arms at waist-high level on your regular walks.

The Bottom Line

*The oxidation of fuel is the foundatin of fat reduction. If you **think oxygen**, you will find more opportunities to **burn fat**.*

My Personal Plan for Day #6

NEGATIVE FORCES
(List any obstacles you must overcome to succeed on Day #6)

_____

_____

_____

_____

_____

POSITIVE ACTIONS
(List the specific steps and plans you will take starting today)

_____

_____

_____

_____

_____

RESULTS
(List changes in your attitude, behavior or physical being due to your actions)

_____

_____

_____

_____

_____

The Week in Review

Day #1: *If you are on a low-calorie diet, it's likely that your body will be out of balance with respect to the essential minerals and vitamins necessary for internal fuel combustion, despite all those diet promises.*

Day #2: *Fast Food is fattening because the greasy stuff slides down so quickly, the **Mind** never has a chance to tell the **Mouth** to shut up.*

Day #3: *By eating slow enough to taste your food, you help prevent overfilling your gas tank at the dinner table.*

Day #4: *Try picturing the symbol C_f (C sub f) to remind yourself: "larger amounts of **carbohydrates** and lower amounts of **fat**."*

Day #5: *Even if you find it impossible to stop eating late-night snacks, reduce the size and percentage of fats in your nighttime meals.*

Day #6: *To approximate how many **calories per minute** you are burning in any given activity, simply note the intensity of your breathing pattern: (1) very heavy: 12-15 calories per minute (cpm) . . . (2) moderately heavy: 7-10 cpm . . . (3) moderate: 4-6 cpm . . . (4) slightly elevated: 2-3 cpm . . . and (5) normal (resting) breathing: 1 cpm.***

**Figures are for a 150-pound person of average metabolism.

Day #7

Walk After Meals

How to Benefit from Post-Meal Walking

Remember the old warning, "Wait an hour after you eat before swimming"?

Perhaps this advice applies to kids stuffed full of french fried fats and greasy burgers. But it's also the perfect plan for gaining weight. Sitting still (resting) after any meal is the trigger habit for a lethargic lifestyle. What follows is **Post-Meal Mortuus** — a drowsy period when your heart pumps extra blood and oxygen to your digestive tract — and you fall asleep at your desk.

To offset **Post-Meal Mortuus**, don't give your body a chance to fall asleep after a meal. Rather, stay active. Not super-active, just moderately so — as in walking!

All you really need do is just walk at a moderate pace for a few minutes after each and every meal. Walking just a few minutes is enough to (1) help digestion, (2) relieve that bloated feeling and (3) burn a few dozen extra calories per meal.

The end results — you'll be more alert after meals . . . your metabolism will stay higher after meals...you'll be less apt to fall asleep in your La-Z-Boy® or office swivel chair.

Thoughts for Day #7

- Walking immediately after a meal is the best remedy for **Post-Meal Mortuus**.

- After a meal, wait at least 10 seconds before walking — just so the food doesn't come dribbling down your lip and chin.

- The difference between sitting still or striding a few minutes after every meal can make a two inch difference on your waistline after a year of 1000 meals.

Objective

- To develop a habit of always taking short, relaxed walks after every meal of your life.

Walk After Meals

The Plan for Day #7

What do you do immediately following the last bite of a meal? Do you slouch back in your dining room chair? Do you clear the table? Do you move to a comfortable couch? If you're in a restaurant, do you start reading the dessert menu or ask to see the dessert cart?

Fact: Each of the post-meal activities mentioned above is fattening. The smart thing to do from a weight control standpoint is to announce in your mind (or out loud), *"Hey folks, the meal is over — it's time to walk!"*

This does not mean a major fitness walking workout. *Post-meal* walks are short, relaxed strolls. They can be as short as two or three minutes or 100 yards. Even two-minute walks are valuable.

Your **Walking Off Weight** goal today is to get up after every meal — and take a short, relaxed walk. Before and after each of these *post-meal walks*, take a moment to record your feelings on the chart below.

Walk After Meals

Time of Meal	Length of Walk	Your Feelings After Your Meal	Your Feelings After Walking
_____(am)	_____(mins)	_____	_____
_____(am)	_____(mins)	_____	_____
_____(am)	_____(mins)	_____	_____
_____(pm)	_____(mins)	_____	_____
_____(pm)	_____(mins)	_____	_____
_____(pm)	_____(mins)	_____	_____

Total Time: _____ (mins) x 5 (cal / min) = _____ **Extra Calories Spent**

At the end of Day #7, review your **Walk-After-Meals** scorecard and total up all the extra post-meal minutes of walking you've done today. Multiply that number by five to calculate your **Extra Caloric Expenditure** for the day. Then divide that number by **10** to approximate your **Net Annual Weight Loss** contribution expected from **Post-Meal Walking.**

Example: Assume you totalled **16** minutes of post-meal walking today. If you maintained this habit regularly for a year, you would burn up:

16 mins x 5 cpm ÷ 10 = 8 pounds per year.

Family Walks: After dinner, invite your entire family to join you as a Walking Team. Start by walking your dishes into the kitchen. Then keep moving — outside. Each day a different family member gets to pick a topic of discussion for the walk.

Imagery: Picture **Walking-After-Meals** as a special kind of dessert — something you really start looking forward to as your meal winds down. This way you'll develop a healthy termination point at the dinner table instead of a painfully tempting and punishing image of 500 calories of cheesecake swimming in strawberry sauce.

Eight Reasons to Walk After Every Meal: (1) Relieves that bloated feeling. (2) Keeps you from falling asleep. (3) Suppresses your desire for dessert. (4) Removes you from the depression of dirty dishes. (5) Gives you renewed energy to do the dishes. (6) Aids digestion. (7) Provides "double-elevated" metabolism (due to simultaneous acts of movement and digestion). (8) Creates new social opportunities and opens communication lines.

Example: The table below shows the net caloric effect of implementing a **Walk-After-Meals** plan. The calculation assumes that in adopting such a plan, you leave the dining table without topping off your meal with *leftovers,* a mouthful of dessert, beverage or something sitting in a candy dish (assumed to be 10 grams or one third of an ounce comprised of 80% sugar and 20% fat with a caloric density of 5 calories per gram.

PER MEAL	(A) EXTRA EXPENDITURE ON 4-MINUTE WALK	→ 20 CALORIE CREDIT
	(B) CALORIC CREDIT FOR NOT "TOPPING OFF" YOUR GAS TANK" (5 cal x 10 grams)	→ 50 CALORIE CREDIT
PER DAY	MULTIPLY (20 + 50) BY 3 MEALS/DAY	→ 210 CALORIE CREDIT
PER YEAR	ASSUME 300 SUCCESSFUL DAYS, 65 UNAVOIDABLE "FAILURES"	→ 63,000 CALORIE CREDIT
FAT REDUCTION	63,000 CALORIE CREDIT / 3,500 CAL/POUND OF FAT	→ 18 POUND WEIGHT LOSS

The Bottom Line

*There are both psychological and physiological reasons to walk after meals. The old philosophy of wait an hour is detrimental to weight loss because it sets you up for Sir Issac Newton's **Law of Inertia: "A body at rest tends to stay at rest."** Once you get into the habit of breaking the inertial force of the **dinner-table-dessert** syndrome, you can live leaner with the more positive version of Sir Issac Newton's **Law of Motion: "A body in motion [after a meal] tends to stay in motion."***

My Personal Plan for Day #7

NEGATIVE FORCES
(List the obstacles you must overcome to succeed on Day # 7)

_____

_____

_____

_____

_____

POSITIVE ACTIONS
(List the specific steps and plans you will take starting today)

_____

_____

_____

_____

_____

RESULTS
(List changes in your attitude, behavior or physical being due to your actions)

_____

_____

_____

_____

_____

The Week in Review

*You have now completed your initial seven days of **Walking Off Weight**. Hopefully you have had a chance to practice the first **seven steps** in **Walking Off Weight** by doing the active exercises for each day as described on pages 15, 21, 27, 33, 39, 45 and 51. To find out how you stand on each of these seven concepts, score yourself in both the **Self-Improvement** and **Absolute Rating** columns.*

		SELF-IMPROVEMENT	ABSOLUTE RATING
		Give yourself the grade which best reflects your improvement for each step.	On a scale of **1 to 10** (10 being perfect), rate yourself for each step by circling a number.
STEP#	DESCRIPTION		
Step 1	**Diets Don't Work**	A B C D	10 9 8 7 6 5 4 3 2 1
Step 2	**Mind, Mouth, Muscle**	A B C D	10 9 8 7 6 5 4 3 2 1
Step 3	**Food is Fuel**	A B C D	10 9 8 7 6 5 4 3 2 1
Step 4	**Go for High-Octane**	A B C D	10 9 8 7 6 5 4 3 2 1
Step 5	**Eat Early**	A B C D	10 9 8 7 6 5 4 3 2 1
Step 6	**Think Oxygen**	A B C D	10 9 8 7 6 5 4 3 2 1
Step 7	**Walk After Meals**	A B C D	10 9 8 7 6 5 4 3 2 1

List below the three steps which you need to practice the most:

(A)_____

(B)_____

(C)_____

Day #8

Walk for Time, Not Speed

Long Slow Distance (LSD) Burns the Fat; High-Speed Walking Burns the Sugar and Stresses the Joints

Whether you walk a mile fast or at a moderate pace, you'll burn about the same number of calories. *Reason:* Going a fixed distance from Point **A** to Point **B** represents a certain amount of work. As long as you get from **A** to **B**, you're going to burn about the same number of calories (assuming your mechanical efficiency does not change considerably at different speeds).

Therefore, the weight-loss lesson to be learned is: *"Walk for time, not speed! Hang in there as long as you can at your most comfortable, enjoyable natural pace."* Remember, four miles of enjoyable walk-talk burns 350 calories for an average 150-pound person. One mile of high-speed sweat-and-strain walking burns only 125 calories. Which workout do you think will let you burn fat consistently over the long haul?

Thoughts for Day #8

- Walking extra miles or extra minutes burns extra fat. Walking extra fast can make your muscles extra sore.

- The race belongs not to the swift.

- You burn about the same number of calories whether you walk from Point **A** to Point **B** quickly or slowly. The key is how far Point **A** is from Point **B**.

- The longer you take to walk a mile, the longer you'll be away from the refrigerator.

- The human body was designed to be a 3.5 miles-per-hour (mph) walking machine.

Objective

- To learn your **optimum walking pace** for fat reduction and weight control.

Walk for Time, Not Speed

The Plan for Day #8

Today's exercise will help you determine your ideal weight-loss walking pace. To accomplish this, you'll need three things: (1) a quarter-mile track (i.e. local high school track), (2) a stopwatch and (3) approximately 20 minutes.

Preliminary: Upon arriving at your high school quarter mile track, sit down and relax for a few minutes. Then measure your resting pulse by placing your second and third fingers lightly on your carotid artery (in the groove of your neck, directly under your jawbone). Count the number of pulses (beats) you feel in six full seconds, and multiply that number by 10 to calculate your pulse (beats per minute).

Lap #1: Slow Lap. Walk one **easy** lap around the 440-yard track at a speed you'd consider slow enough to be a warm-up pace. Monitor the time it takes you to complete this lap and measure your walking heart rate immediately upon finishing. Record your lap time and pulse on the chart below.

Lap #2: Fast Lap. Walk one **very fast** lap of the track. Again, time yourself and record your lap time and pulse at the end of the lap.

Lap #3: Medium Lap. Walk one moderate-paced lap of the track. Again time yourself and record your walking heart rate at the end of your lap.

	1/4-MILE TIME	HEART RATE
Slow Lap (#1)	_____min _____sec	_____ Beats Per Minute
Fast Lap (#2)	_____min _____sec	_____ Beats Per Minute
Med. Lap (#3)	_____min _____sec	_____ Beats Per Minute

Conclusion. Your *ideal weight-loss walking speed* is the pace you walked on your final lap (medium pace). One way to double check this, is to see if your walking heart rate was close to **55%** to **65%** of your maximum estimated heart rate. This check can be made as follows:

Step 1: Calculate your estimated maximum heart rate by subtracting your age from the number 220. **Example:** If you're 40, your maximum heart rate is approximated as **220 - 40 = 180**.

Step 2: Multiply your Maximum Heart Rate by **55%** and **65%** respectively to find your **target range** for weight-loss walking. **Example:** If you're 40, your **target range** is 99 BPM (55% of 180) to 117 BPM (65% of 180).

Step 3: Check the heart rate you achieved at the end of your medium-paced lap. If it falls in the 100-120 BPM range (for middle-aged people), you're right on target. If it's a little **lower** than 100, it means you have room to pick the pace up a bit. If it's **higher** than 120, slow down a bit.

NOTE: These target heart rates for weight-loss walking are about 10% to 15% less than the standard target heart rates you may be accustomed to for cardiovascular conditioning.

Example: John is 20 years old and 20 pounds overweight. Other than that, he is relatively healthy. **Question:** What target heart range should he train at for comfortable, consistent weight-loss walking?

Step 1 Estimate John's maximum heart rate: **MHR = 220 - 20 = 200 BPM**
Step 2 Multiply John's MHR by **55%** and **65%** to find his lower and upper limits: **55% (200) = 110 BPM   65% (200) = 130 BPM**

Answer: If John walked at a pace which raised his heart rate up to **110 to 130 BPM**, then most likely he'd be working out at a comfortable, fat-burning, conversational pace.

Creative Ideas for Day #8

- Walk one lap of a quarter-mile track at what you think is a 3.5 mph pace. If you're on target, you'll finish in 4 minutes, 17 seconds. If you finish either 10 seconds (or more) too slow or too fast, try again until you're reasonably close. Ask yourself if 3.5 mph feels comfortable. As it turns out, over 90% of all walkers feel very much at ease walking at a 3.5 mph pace (a 17 minute mile).

- Identify two objects in your neighborhood that are about 100 yards apart (approximately the length of a football field). Stand alongside one object and time yourself on **how fast** you can walk to the other object. Then, time yourself on an **easier more natural** walk back. Think about how each walk felt. Finally ask yourself: *"Which of these two paces would I choose if I were going out on a long, fat-burning weight-loss walk?"* Remember, both walks burn about the same number of calories.

The Bottom Line

The human body was designed to be a 3.5 mph walking machine. If you want to burn fat, learn the art of medium-paced walking. In other words, walk at a comfortable 3.5 mph pace, without pain and strain, and for relatively long distances and long periods of time. For the non-athletic population wishing to shed weight, walking between 3.3 and 3.7 mph will do the trick!

My Personal Plan for Day #8

NEGATIVE FORCES
(List any obstacles you must overcome to succeed on Day #8)

_____

_____

_____

_____

_____

POSITIVE ACTIONS
(List the specific steps and plans you will take starting today)

_____

_____

_____

_____

_____

RESULTS
(List changes in your attitude, behavior or physical being due to your actions)

_____

_____

_____

_____

_____

The Week in Review

Day #7: *The walk from the dinner table to the La-Z-Boy® is the kiss of death in weight loss. It burns only one calorie and sets you up for a night of fat-making lethargy.*

Day #8: *If you're sore with stiff muscles the day after one of your weight-loss walks, you're probably pushing the pace too much. The soreness may be due to residual pools of lactic acid (the by-product of vigorous anaerobic exercise) trapped in the muscles. By slowing down to train aerobically, your muscles will burn fat in the presence of oxygen — without generating significant amounts of lactic acid.*

Be A Swinger

Learning the Value of Arm Swing in Weight-Loss Walking

The two most underrated *players* on your walking team are your *right* and *left arms*. These limbs swing to and fro some 100 to 140 times per minute, providing both rhythm and balance. They also make an important contribution to your speed and caloric expenditure.

If you walk without any arm swing, you're probably burning *25% less* calories. Just swinging your arms moderately at your sides will *improve* your energy expenditure by at least *10%*. It's that easy.

Basically there are two ways to swing your arms: **(1) Pendulum Style** — at your sides (arms fully extended), and **(2) Right Angle-Bent** (arms cocked, with forearm and biceps perpendicular). The **Right-Angle** technique is more *powerful*; it'll make you go faster and help you burn more calories. It may also make you feel more self-conscious. The **Pendulum** technique is much more *natural* and *comfortable*, especially for the more self-conscious walker.

The easy way to find out which arm swing motion is best for you is to play a game of trial and error. That's what Day #9 is all about — learning what type of *swinger* you want to be.

Thoughts for Day #9

- The more large muscle groups you put into motion, the more fat you're going to burn.

- A high-energy arm swing can help you burn 25% more calories (than no arm swing). At a half-hour a day of walking, that can add up to 15,000 extra calories a year — or four pounds less of body fat.

- The most inefficient, non-ideal arm swing still burns plenty of extra calories.

Objectives

- To appreciate the value of your arm swing in *Walking Off Weight*.

- To learn your ideal arm-swing technique.

Be A Swinger

The Plan for Day #*9*

Today is *Arm-Swing Day*. To commemorate it, you'll have a chance to take **three walks**, each lasting **one whole minute**. In each walk, you will use your arms differently to demonstrate the impact of different arm-swing technique. This exercise will help you appreciate the **value** of arm-swing and which **style** of arm swing suits you best. You will need: an open walking area, a stopwatch, a colorful piece of cloth and 10 minutes of time.

First, select a clear path on which to walk. The following areas can work well: a neighborhood sidewalk, a local high school track, an open grass field or a quiet road with a wide shoulder for walking. Once you've selected a site, clearly identify an official starting line from which to begin all three of your one-minute arm-swing walks.

Walk 1: No Arm Swing

From the start line, walk as reasonably fast as you can — but with both hands clasped together in front of you. Check your stopwatch occasionally and stop walking after 60 seconds have elapsed. (If you undershoot or overshoot by a few seconds, correct your distance by walking forwards or backwards a total of TWO steps for every second you were off). Mark your progress with a colored cloth and measure the distance you covered in a minute by simply counting how many steps it takes you to walk back to the start line. Then, prepare for Walk #2.

Walk 2: High-Energy Pendulum Arm Swing

Repeat the one-minute walk. However, this time swing your arms **pendulum style** with all of your energy. Once again, walk for one minute. On returning to your starting point, count how many footsteps you walked *past* Marker #1. Return for Walk #3.

Walk 3: High-Energy Bent-Arm Swing

Repeat the one-minute walk, but this time bend your arms in a **Right-Angle** configuration such that your forearms and biceps are perpendicular to each other. Keep your elbows moving horizontally in a plane parallel to the ground (approximately 6" to 12" above your waist). Put all your energy into this back and forth pumping arm swing, while maintaining the same intensity level as in your two previous walks. Measure your distance by counting the footsteps back to your starting point.

After Walk #3: Check out the effect of arm swing by measuring how far you walked in a minute. Complete the chart below. Then ask yourself, *"Which style am I most comfortable with on a long-term basis?"*

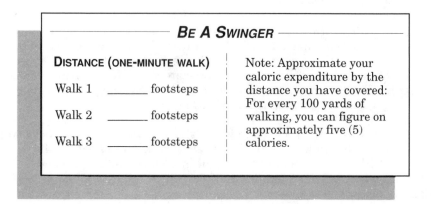

BE A SWINGER

DISTANCE (ONE-MINUTE WALK)

Walk 1 _____ footsteps

Walk 2 _____ footsteps

Walk 3 _____ footsteps

Note: Approximate your caloric expenditure by the distance you have covered: For every 100 yards of walking, you can figure on approximately five (5) calories.

Example

Mary just completed her first series of Arm-Swing Walks on a country road. Her results are tabulated below.

Walk #1	**80 yards in a minute**	**100 footsteps**
Walk #2	**92 yards in a minute**	**116 footsteps**
Walk #3	**100 yards in a minute**	**125 footsteps**

In reviewing her performances, Mary realizes that she covered 25% more distance and spent 25% more calories using the high-energy, **Right-Angle** arm swing (Walk #3) compared to **no** arm swing (Walk #1). However, she felt somewhat self-conscious pumping her arms during Walk #3. Yet, she didn't feel uneasy during her **Pendulum** arm-swing walk (Walk #2). After taking everything into account, Mary feels most satisfied using a **Pendulum** arm-swing style, at a fairly high-energy level (Walk #2).

The Bottom Line

*As long as you include some style of arm-swing into your walking gait, you're going to burn more calories and move along with better rhythm. Select the arm-swing technique which feels **right for you**, regardless of how fast it enables you to walk.*

My Personal Plan for Day #9

NEGATIVE FORCES
(List any obstacles you must overcome to succeed on Day #9)

_____

_____

_____

_____

_____

_____

POSITIVE ACTIONS
(List the specific steps and plans you will take starting today)

_____

_____

_____

_____

_____

RESULTS
(List changes in your attitude, behavior or physical being due to your actions)

_____

_____

_____

_____

_____

_____

The Week in Review

Day #7: *A one-mile easy walk after meals is great; but even three-minute strolls help.*

Day #8: *Three and a half miles per hour walking is the best overall pace for most people. It's perfect for children (9 years and up); it's great for adults on a weight-loss program. Plus, it's beneficial for many senior walkers.*

Day #9: *Swaying your arms from side to side (as opposed to swaying them to and fro) will help you keep a rhythmic walking gait, and because it's inefficient, it will burn extra calories. Most walkers, however, prefer not to be seen swaying their arms like a gorilla.*

The Magic Walking Formula: Ten Two's (2222-222-22-2)

How 2222-222-22-2 Can Help You Design Your Walking Weight Loss Exercise Program

What is the best kept secret in Walking Prescriptions? Try **Ten Two's**. Otherwise known as **2222-222-22-2**. Just study the inverted pyramid below to see how you can fit 2222-222-22-2 into your life.

2	2	2	2	**2222**	**Calories** *of walking per* **week**
	2	2	2	**222**	**Hours** *of walking per* **year**
		2	2	**22**	**Miles** *of walking per* **week**
			2	**2**	**Minutes** *of extra* **life** *for every* **minute** *of* **walking**

Conclusion: If you can build your walking program up to the approximate levels shown in the **Ten Two's Inverted Pyramid**, you'll significantly reduce your risk of heart disease (based on data from *The Harvard Alumni Study* which indicated that alumni expending 2000-2500 extra calories in various forms of physical activity lived longer, healthier lives). At the same time, a weekly expenditure in the range of 2,000 to 2,500 calories (or 2,222 calories) will help you burn an extra two-thirds of a pound of body fat per week. This translates to an average of approximately **three miles** of walking per day.

Thoughts for Day #10

- For every minute you walk, you can extend your life by as much as two minutes.

- If the sedentary population of the United States could spend an extra 2000 to 2500 calories of energy walking per week, this country would see a lot less heart attacks and by-pass surgery. We'd also take up a bit *less space* on this crowded planet.

Objective

- To learn simple ways to prescribe the proper amounts of walking necessary to lose weight and stay healthy.

The Magic Walking Formula: Ten Two's 2222-222-22-2

The Plan for Day #10

IF you consistently walk 20 – 25 miles weekly, your chances of reducing both your **body weight** and **cardiovascular risk** will improve.

Although it could take several months (or more) to build up to 20 – 25 miles of walking per week, your goal today is to see how close you can come to this level of mileage. Consistent with the **Ten Two's Formula** (2222-222-22-2), try to log 22 miles of walking each week as your long-term goal. To help you realize your progress and to put a little childish play into your walking program, two scorekeeping games — **Charlie the Caterpillar** and **The Walking Piggy Bank** — are offered for your fun and enjoyment.

Charlie the Caterpillar: Charlie is a caterpillar who likes to walk. Every time he covers a mile, he gets one section of his white furry body dyed gray (Charlie has 22 sections). His weekly goal is to become totally gray. He then gets a new shag haircut to remove all his grown-out gray hairs so that he can start his next 22-mile week of walking with a clean slate of fresh white fur.

Use Charlie, the Walking Caterpillar, as a visual graph to record your weekly walking miles (target goal: 22 miles per week).

Starting today, begin walking with Charlie (don't worry, he'll maintain your pace). But since you don't have 22 sections of white fur to dye, we're giving you a picture of Charlie to color in. For every mile you walk, shade in one of Charlie's 22 sections. In seven days, see how many sections (miles) you have shaded. Ultimately, try to keep pace with Charlie at 22 miles per week.

The Walking Piggy Bank Game: Starting today, if you were to deposit 10 cents in a **Piggy Bank** for every mile you walked, how much money would you save by the end of the week? If you hit the 22-mile goal, you'd be putting away $2.20 a week. The nice thing about this game is that you don't have to worry about logbooks or recordkeeping. All you need to do is drop one dime in your homemade **Piggy Bank** for each mile you walked that day. At the end of the week, open up your **Piggy Bank** and count your change. If you hit $2.20, you're right on target. Then start the next week off with a clean slate. By depositing your weekly **Piggy Bank** savings, you could wind up with a *cumulative walking dividend* of 52 x $2.20 or **$114.40** saved in one year of walking.

Alternative Game: Lost-and-Found

In addition to your **Piggy Bank** collection, keep a **Lost-and-Found Jar** to hold all the loose change you find along the streets as you walk. You'd be surprised how the pennies, nickles and dimes add up. Realize that if you averaged even 10 cents a day on your walks, you'd collect **$36.50** a year just from coin prospecting in the streets. That's about enough to buy a new pair of walking shoes — on sale.

The Bottom Line

*There are many ways to average 20 –25 miles of walking per week. You can walk about 3 miles a day, seven days a week (21 miles). Or you can do shorter walks during the mid-week (2-mile walks) and longer ones on the weekends (5- to 6-milers). From an aerobic conditioning standpoint, it helps if you alternate your **hard** walking workouts (high-speed, high-intensity, shorter duration) with your **easy** workouts (lower-speed, longer duration). However, from a weight-loss standpoint, the most important thing is that you burn calories on a consistent daily and weekly basis. Either way — **22 miles** or **2222 calories** — is a good target to shoot for weekly.*

My Personal Plan for Day #10

NEGATIVE FORCES
(List any obstacles you must overcome to succeed on Day #10)

_____

_____

_____

_____

_____

_____

POSITIVE ACTIONS
(List the specific steps and plans you will take starting today)

_____

_____

_____

_____

_____

_____

RESULTS
(List changes in your attitude, behavior or physical being due to your actions)

_____

_____

_____

_____

_____

_____

The Week in Review

Day #7: Post-meal *walks should not* steal *too much blood and oxygen from the digestive system. Hence, it's best to walk at a moderate pace and intensity immediately after eating.*

Day #8: *Very fast walking can lead to injury or muscle soreness. If you slow down to a more comfortable pace, you'll stay out there longer, burn more fat and have more fun.*

Day #9: *Heavy hands make for a distorted arm swing. Plus, they do little to increase caloric expenditure and heart-rate levels. If you really want to use weights to significantly increase your energy expenditure, you'd need to wear a lead vest weighing 30 or more pounds (25% of body weight). Is it worth it?*

Day #10: *If you hit your target goal of **2,222** calories per week . . . realize that's approximately 115,000 calories per year. Divide 115,000 by 3,500 calories per pound of fat—and you'll have spent **33 extra pounds of fat** for walking fuel this year.*

Walk Eight Days a Week

The Justification for Walking Every Day of the Week — and More

If we really believe that exercise is vital to healthy living, why shouldn't we do it daily? If it caused pain or muscle inflammation or aching joints, yes — then you could argue against daily punishment. But walking? No way! In fact, on days when time permits, you might even walk twice.

If you expect to lose weight, it really helps to integrate at least one period of physical activity (such as walking) into your daily regimen. It's the cumulative effect of consistent aerobic activity that will help you burn off your stores of body fat. The time of day you walk isn't as important as maintaining a consistent schedule.

Walking eight days (or eight times) a week guarantees you'll get seven workouts done in a week — even if you miss a day occasionally.

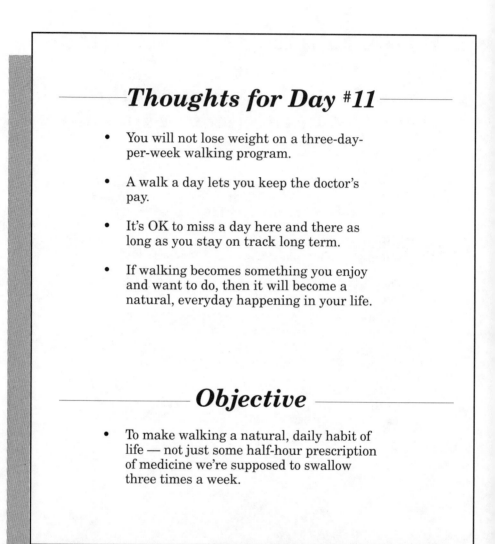

Thoughts for Day #11

- You will not lose weight on a three-day-per-week walking program.

- A walk a day lets you keep the doctor's pay.

- It's OK to miss a day here and there as long as you stay on track long term.

- If walking becomes something you enjoy and want to do, then it will become a natural, everyday happening in your life.

Objective

- To make walking a natural, daily habit of life — not just some half-hour prescription of medicine we're supposed to swallow three times a week.

Walk Eight Days a Week

The Plan for Day #11

Most successful walkers have one thing in common — a consistent time of the day set aside for their walks. This *time slot* varies from person to person, and no one time is better than another. It's what works for you.

Interestingly, you may not know what time of day really works best for you. That's why on **Day #11** of *Walking Off Weight* your assignment is to figure out your body's natural affinity for walking in the **morning**, **afternoon** and **evening**.

To start with, assume nothing. Show no favoritism or prejudice towards any part of the day. Just say to yourself, *"I'm going to give each segment of the day an equal shot for walking and judge each walk based on how I feel."*

The Morning Walk

For openers, pick a time slot in the morning. For you, this may mean walking right after waking up or after eating breakfast — or after showering (the walk need not be sweat producing). Perhaps you'd enjoy walking 15 to 20 minutes at work by arriving there early (and missing the morning rush hour in the process). During and after your walk, think about the positive and negative aspects of taking **morning** walks. Finally, after completing your morning walk, record your feelings below.

Walk Time	Positive Feelings	Negative Feelings
MORNING _____AM		
AFTERNOON _____PM		
EVENING _____PM		

The Afternoon Walk

Later on today, repeat this procedure by taking a second walk — right around lunchtime. During this walk, contemplate the *pros* and *cons* of lunchtime walking **for you** and then record your thoughts.

The Evening Walk

Finally, and regardless of your reactions to your **morning** and **afternoon** walks, take a third walk later in the day — say between 5 p.m. and 10 p.m. Again, record your thoughts on the chart.

After recording all your thoughts, start reflecting on **what works best for you**. If you're still undecided about **two times** of the day, do a few follow-up walks this week until **one time** emerges as the outright **winner**. Let your second favorite time serve as your back-up.

The Pros and Cons of Walking at Different Times of the Day

Early Morning Advantages: Least interference from the day's activities ■ Establishes elevated metabolism for remainder of the morning ■ Energizes you for morning tasks.

Early Morning Disadvantages: Must conquer the snooze alarm clock ■ Body is relatively stiff and requires the greatest warm-up.

Lunchtime Advantages: Picks you up at your lowest energy level of the day ■ Does not add time to your workday ■ Helps you from overeating at lunch ■ Relieves office frustration and stress.

Lunchtime Disadvantages: Meetings and appointments often can upset the regularity of your walking program.

Late Afternoon-Evening Advantages: Great for relieving end-of-the-day stress ■ Body is naturally warmed up and loose ■ Family can participate ■ Keeps you away from the refrigerator and TV ■ Helps cut late-night snacking.

Late Afternoon-Evening Disadvantages: Requires prioritizing with other nighttime activities ■ Can interfere with sleep if done right before bedtime.

The Bottom Line

*To be successful at **Walking Off Weight**, you need to walk on a consistent, daily basis — at least **"eight" days a week**. For that to happen, develop a walking schedule suitable to your lifestyle and liking. By sampling a variety of walks at different times of the day, your **mind** and **body** can judge what's best for you.*

My Personal Plan for Day #11

NEGATIVE FORCES
(List the obstacles you must overcome to succeed on Day #11)

_____

_____

_____

_____

_____

_____

POSITIVE ACTIONS
(List the specific steps you will take starting today)

_____

_____

_____

_____

_____

_____

RESULTS
(List changes in your attitude, behavior or physical being due to your actions)

_____

_____

_____

_____

_____

_____

The Week in Review

Day #8: *By walking at a 3.5 mph pace, a 150-pound person burns approximately five calories every minute. In front of the TV, that same person burns one calorie per minute. That's why every minute you walk counts in the **Weight Loss** game.*

Day #9: *You can burn 20 extra calories per mile by simply increasing the energy of your arm swing.*

Day #10: *Research data from the Harvard Alumni Study shows that by spending 2000 to 2,500 calories per week in a walking program, the average middle-aged person extends his or her life by two years.*

Day #11: *Walking eight days a week doesn't mean you need to find time for eight 45-minute workouts. Just try to get some walking in every day. Even short, 10-minute walks count on your **Caloric Scoreboard**.*

M&M's Are Really Football Fields

How Far Would You Need to Walk to Burn Off One M&M?

The energy stored in **one M&M** is enough to fuel a 150-pound walker across a football field. Both end zones included.

This may not impress you — until you stand at one goal post gazing 120 yards across a sea of grass at the other goal post with a tiny M&M clutched in your fist. That should help you appreciate the physical effort necessary to burn off the little sugar-coated ellipsoid of chocolate.

There's a lesson to be learned here in Hersheyland: what **melts** in your mouth must ultimately be burned up. Otherwise, it **melts** a second time inside your fat cells.

Up to now you may have thought of M&M's as a special treat, a reward or a topping. And they really are all of those. But they are also **football fields** [of potential energy] in disguise.

Thoughts for Day #12

- If it takes one football field of walking to burn off one M&M, what would it take to burn off a Big Mac, fries and a shake? *Answer:* **240 football fields**. That's *five hours* of straight walking!

- By walking one football field, you burn off one M&M (a one-minute walk). Try 55 football fields (55 minutes) for the small 45¢ bag of Plain M&M's.

Objective

- To understand the human energy balance, and that it takes **one football field** of walking (end zones included) to burn off **one** M&M.

M&M's Are Really Football Fields

The Plan for Day #*12*

Today you're going to take a trip to your local high school football field. On the way, though, you'll need to make one small shopping detour. Stop off and buy a small bag of plain M&M's. That's the little, dark-brown 45¢ bag — **not** the large brown or large yellow bag costing $1.98.

Next, drive or walk from the store to the football field with the bag of M&M's locked in your car trunk or zipped up in your jacket. If you open them prematurely you'll ruin this entire exercise (plus you'll gain 10 pounds instantly for disobedience).

Upon arriving at the football field, walk your bag of M&M's to the back line of one of the end zones (10 yards behind the goal line). Finally, tear off the corner of the bag and push out **one** and **only one** M&M candy into the palm of your hand. Put the bag away — out of sight, out of reach — temporarily. Now, stare at the one M&M in your palm for a few seconds and think how it will taste melting in your mouth. Then eat the M&M your favorite way. Yummy, yummy. Right?

Now, stare straight out over the entire length of the football field. That's how far you're going to have to walk to burn off the **one M&M** you've just eaten. **One football field — end zones included**. One hundred and twenty (120) yards!

Walk it! Yes, walk it! One football field. And don't forget to keep the rest of the bag **locked** in your pocket.

Upon arriving at the other end of the football field (you just scored a touchdown by the way), take out your bag of M&M's and squeeze out just **one more** M&M. Again, stare at it for a while. Then, look back over the entire grass field you just walked. Then stare back at the **M&M**; then the **football field**. Finally ask yourself: *"If I eat this M&M (M&M #2), would I be willing to walk the length of this field again?"*

If your answer is *"yes,"* eat **M&M #2**, and walk **one more football field**. If your answer is *"no,"* the game is over and you can throw your M&M's in the nearest garbage receptacle and return home. Don't feel bad; 45¢ is a cheap price to pay for an entire session in weight control.

But let's assume you were ambitious enough to *walk off* **M&M #2**. If so, take out **M&M #3** after returning to your original starting point at the end of the football field. Once again, ask yourself, *"Am I willing to walk another football field for another M&M?"*

Repeat this procedure as many times as your **Mouth**, **Muscles** and **Mind** are willing to agree on.

Final Note

If you elect to take this exercise to its final endpoint, be prepared to walk about 55 lengths of the football field. That's how many M&M's are in a small 45¢ bag of Plain. That translates to about 3.3 miles of walking — a tough price to pay for a few minutes of junk-food indulgence.

The Bottom Line

Don't get scared! Not all the food we eat needs to be walked off. That's because in the normal course of daily living your basal resting metabolism operates at 800 to 1200 calories (per day) — just to maintain normal body functions. However, it's the extra little treats we need to be concerned about. Like that little **chocolate chip cookie (8 football fields)** *. . . or that scoop of* **ice-cream** *drenched in viscous syrup (50 football fields) . . . or that extra slice of* **pepperoni pizza** *on the boardwalk (60 football fields) . . . or that Big Mac (100 football fields). That's why we need to appreciate that something as small as an M&M is really as large as a* **football field.**

My Personal Plan for Day #12

NEGATIVE FORCES
(List the obstacles you must overcome to succeed on Day #12)

_____

_____

_____

_____

_____

_____

POSITIVE ACTIONS
(List the specific steps you will take starting today)

_____

_____

_____

_____

_____

RESULTS
(List changes in your attitude, behavior, or physical being due to your actions)

_____

_____

_____

_____

_____

_____

The Week in Review

Day #8: *One barometer for calibrating your walking speed is to converse with a friend during a fairly brisk walk. When breathing becomes difficult and your conversation starts to halt, you've just exceeded your ideal weight-loss pace. Back off a bit until it's reasonably comfortable to talk again.*

Day #9: *By swinging your arms in a slightly higher arc, and by occasionally raising them up in the air over your shoulder (**for short periods**), you can relieve the uncomfortable swelling that often occurs in the fingers. As you become more aerobically conditioned, this swollen-hand syndrome will become less bothersome.*

Day #10: *If you exceed the **2000 to 2500** calorie-per-week level in exercise, that's even better from a weight-loss standpoint. If you consistently push yourself beyond **3,500** calories a week in aerobic activity, you will burn more calories. But your cardiovascular risk actually increases somewhat when compared to a more rational **2000 to 2500** calorie approach to exercise. **Conclusion**: You receive most of the **cardiovascular** and **weight loss** benefits simply by burning a **consistent 2000 to 2500** calories per week.*

Day #11: *One way to lose weight by walking **three** days a week is to substitute an equivalent aerobic activity for walking on alternate days. As long as the **intensity** and **duration** of that alternative exercise are equivalent to your walking, caloric expenditures will be about the same. Realize though, **success** still depends on doing **daily** aerobic exericse.*

Day #12: *If walking the length of **one football field** burns off **one Plain M&M**, how many football fields of walking does it take to burn off a **Peanut M & M**? Answer: **two football fields**. The peanut alone is worth a second football field [five calories].*

Little Changes Make Big Differences

In Weight Management, It's the Little, Everyday Things You Do (or Don't Do) That Count in the Long Haul

Rome wasn't built in a day and neither was your body. So be patient. **Successful** weight loss is **slow** weight loss. **Fast** weight loss is **foolish** and **fruitless**.

Of the 20 million Americans on diets, most would be extremely pleased if they could lose 52 pounds the first year. That's only **one** pound per week. Sound easy? Try it! Then report back to us after 52 weeks and we'll see if you averaged a pound a week.

The point is that you don't have to become a fitness fanatic or a marathon runner to lose weight. All you need to do is work on the **details of daily living** — those little handfuls of chocolate-chip cookies and the extra slabs of butter on the pancakes — or the little midnight sleepwalking trips to the freezer full of frozen Snickers and ice-cream. It all adds up and usually in the wrong direction.

Thoughts for Day #13

- *"A journey of a thousand miles starts with a single step."* —Lao Tse

- Walking up one extra flight of stairs a day can save you a half pound of fat in a year.

- The electric typewriter has cost the average American secretary one and a half extra pounds of body fat per year.

- Eating **three** little M&M's (15 calories) a day will put one and a half extra pounds of body fat on you in a year. That's **15 pounds** extra fat in a decade.

- None of us need to become jocks to lose weight. It's the **little** things we do or don't do in a day that ultimately determine our weight and waistline.

Objective

- To learn to appreciate the principle that **little lifestyle changes** add up to **big weight loss accomplishments**.

Little Changes Make Big Differences

The Plan for Day #13

Today is officially titled **Little Changes Day**, because in the course of the next 24 hours your task is to make many **little lifestyle changes** conducive to sensible weight loss. For each **little change** you make, approximate the yearlong impact of that change on your weight. For example, if you decided to add a five-minute pre-breakfast walk to your morning routine each workday, that would help you burn approximately **5 minutes** x **5 calories per minute** x **210 workdays** per year or **5250 extra calories** per year. That's enough to burn up **1.5 pounds** of fat.

To aid you in your efforts today, a special scorecard is provided below. As a goal today, see if you can make **5 little changes** in your lifestyle that will help you be fitter and leaner tomorrow. To gain a better understanding of the **caloric consequences** of your **little changes**, check out the table on the next page.

Your Little Changes

Description of Your Little Changes	Daily Caloric Impact	Yearly Caloric Impact	Annual Weight Loss (Estimated)
(1)			
(2)			
(3)			
(4)			
(5)			
Total Weight Loss Impact ⟶			

Description of Your Little Changes	Daily Caloric Impact	Yearly Caloric Impact	Annual Weight Loss (Estimated)
• Climb one extra flight of stairs	5	1750	0.5
• Leave one slab of butter off the pancakes or baked potatoes	30	10,500	3.0
• Walk in your neighborhood until you find a penny (10 mins. avg.)	50	17,500	5.0
• Manually operate your TV	6	2100	0.6
• Loop the living room every time you change a channel	10	3500	1.0
• Give up your evening candy or ice-cream treat during TV news	200	70,000	20.0
• Pull 10 weeds from your garden	10	3500	1.0
• Park 100 extra yards away from your work entrance	5	1750	0.5
• Stoop to pick up a few soda cans	3	1000	0.3
• Walk one minute after each meal	15	5250	1.5
• Rise up and stretch 5x at work	8	2800	0.8
• Eat twice as slowly by placing your fork down after each bite	20	7000	2.0
• Substitute one stick of celery for one sucking candy	10	3500	1.0
• Replace one fatty food with one carbohydrate-rich food	100	35,000	10.0
• Walk 8 extra minutes a day	40	14,000	4.0
• Walk 12 extra minutes a day	60	21,000	6.0
• Walk 15 extra minutes a day	80	28,000	8.0
• Cut your own lawn 20x a year	400	8000	2.3
• One less donut per week	200	10,000	2.8
• One less ice-cream cone per week	200	10,000	2.8
• Five less tablespoons of salad dressing per week	300	15,000	4.3
• Walk one extra stop before hopping on the bus	25	8500	2.5
• Eat three less M&M's per day	15	5250	1.5
Total Weight Loss Credit:		**284,900 Calories**	**81.4 Pounds**

The Bottom Line

*As you can see, it doesn't take a lot. Either way, from a **plus or minus** stand-point, the **little** changes can make or break us. You don't need to go overboard. Simply focus on a few positive lifestyle changes — and stay with them. It's like opening up a new savings account. Except in **Walking Off Weight**, you try to make steady withdrawals instead of deposits.*

My Personal Plan for Day #13

NEGATIVE FORCES
(List the obstacles you must overcome to succeed on Day #13)

_____

_____

_____

_____

_____

POSITIVE ACTIONS
(List the specific steps you will take starting today)

_____

_____

_____

_____

_____

RESULTS
(List changes in your attitude, behavior, or physical being due to these actions)

_____

_____

_____

_____

_____

The Week in Review

You have now completed your initial **14 days** of **Walking Off Weight**. Hopefully you have had a chance to put into practice the **14 steps** for successful weight management. To find out how you stand on each of these **14** concepts, score yourself in both the **Self-Improvement** and **Absolute Rating** columns.

STEP#	DESCRIPTION	SELF-IMPROVEMENT Give yourself the grade which reflects your improvement over the past two weeks for each step.	ABSOLUTE RATING On a scale of **1 to 10** (10 being perfect) rate yourself for each step by circling a number.
Step 1	**Diets Don't Work**	A B C D	10 9 8 7 6 5 4 3 2 1
Step 2	**Mind-Mouth-Muscle**	A B C D	10 9 8 7 6 5 4 3 2 1
Step 3	**Food is Fuel**	A B C D	10 9 8 7 6 5 4 3 2 1
Step 4	**Go for High Octane**	A B C D	10 9 8 7 6 5 4 3 2 1
Step 5	**Eat Early**	A B C D	10 9 8 7 6 5 4 3 2 1
Step 6	**Think Oxygen**	A B C D	10 9 8 7 6 5 4 3 2 1
Step 7	**Walk After Meals**	A B C D	10 9 8 7 6 5 4 3 2 1
Step 8	**Walk for Time . . .**	A B C D	10 9 8 7 6 5 4 3 2 1
Step 9	**Be A Swinger**	A B C D	10 9 8 7 6 5 4 3 2 1
Step10	**The Magic Formula . . .**	A B C D	10 9 8 7 6 5 4 3 2 1
Step11	**Walk 8 Days A Week**	A B C D	10 9 8 7 6 5 4 3 2 1
Step12	**M&M's Are . . .**	A B C D	10 9 8 7 6 5 4 3 2 1
Step13	**Little Changes . . .**	A B C D	10 9 8 7 6 5 4 3 2 1
Step14	**Take The "P" Test**	A B C D	10 9 8 7 6 5 4 3 2 1

Take the "P - Test"

Focusing Only on Those Walking and Weight Loss Habits You'd Be Willing to Stick to for Life

Almost all dieters consistently regain their lost weight (plus additional fat) because they return to their old ways of eating and living. This tendency accounts for hundreds of millions of pounds of cyclic fat loss and fat gain each year — not to mention the billions of dollars wasted on diet programs.

If you're really serious about weight loss, you need to ask yourself one critical question before you make any life-style change: **"Am I truly willing to live by this change for the rest of my life?"**

If your answer is **no**, you're wasting your time. If your answer is **yes**, you've passed the *P-Test*. As you may have already guessed, *P* stands for *Permanent*.

If you take the *P-Test* and answer honestly, then you're going to save a lot of money and frustration.

Thoughts for Day #14

- There's really no sense in making lifestyle changes for weight loss unless you're ready to commit to those changes long-term.

- Before you decide on changing a habit, take the *P-Test*. If your answer is *Yes*, then go with that change.

Objective

- To learn how to use the *P-Test* to decide on healthy lifestyle changes which you can live with the rest of your life.

Take the "P - Test"

The Plan for Day #14 —————————————————————

On Day #13, you were very brave to write down all the **little changes** you'd be willing to make as part of your **Walking Off Weight** personal action plan.

Now get serious! Go back over your list of little changes. Individually review each item on your chart. For each item listed, take the *P-Test*.

For Example: If you doubt that you'll be able to maintain a particular action plan for very long — scratch it! Then go onto the next item. If it passes the *P-Test*, transcribe that change onto your new list below. Also show the specific caloric impact of each item. Now, add up all of your individual **little changes** to arrive at a **total** anticipated impact as predicted on your **caloric scoreboard** below.

Little Changes That Pass the "P-Test"			
Description of Your Little Changes	Daily Caloric Impact	Yearly Caloric Impact	Annual Weight Loss (Estimated)
(1)			
(2)			
(3)			
(4)			
(5)			
Total Weight Loss Impact ——▶			

Suggestions

1. If you're having trouble deciding on whether you're really committed to a change permanently, go out on a walk and think about it. Just be honest with yourself. This is a game between you, your conscience and your waistline.

2. If you answer **no** on a *P-Test* for a particular item, reconsider by asking yourself, *"Am I chewing off too much?"* Maybe your **little** change is too **big** a change. What if you chose a smaller goal, something you're confident you'd stick with? You can always increase your goal later.

3. In taking the *P-Test*, realize that nothing in this world or in your life is truly permanent. Everything changes. Sure, you're going to drift off course occasionally. But the **real** question to ask yourself is, ***"On a long-term basis, is this the kind of lifestyle change that I'll ultimately keep coming back to?"***

The Bottom Line

In any weight loss program, consistency and persistence win out over everything else. Those who think they're in the weight loss game for quick gains (i.e. quick weight loss) will be long term losers. Those who answer honestly in the **P-Test** *and make lifelong commitments to little changes, will develop permanent habits and nurture attitudes that lead to enjoyment, self-satisfaction and painless weight control.*

My Personal Plan for Day #14

NEGATIVE FORCES
(List the obstacles you must overcome to succeed on Day #14)

_____

_____

_____

_____

_____

_____

POSITIVE ACTIONS
(List the specific steps you will take starting today)

_____

_____

_____

_____

_____

RESULTS
(List changes in your attitude, behavior, or physical being due to these actions)

_____

_____

_____

_____

_____

On the 15th Day

For the last 14 days of **Walking Off Weight** you have been a student of *walking, nutrition, exercise physiology* and *lifestyle planning*. You have learned the truth about diets, the value of high-octane fuels and the best speeds to walk for weight loss. You've also learned that *M & M's are football fields.*

Now it's Day #15 — *Graduation Day* — and it's time to put your knowledge to work. As you can see, when you finish reading this page, you're out of workbook. Yet your **Walking Off Weight** program is far from over. In fact, it never ends. These 14 steps should last you a lifetime. Some will come very naturally. Others will take much more practice to perfect. The better you get at them, the easier you'll shed unwanted fat.

Right now, you might be concerned because you probably haven't dropped much weight since beginning this book. Actually, that's great! Save the weight loss for the months ahead. For now, it's more important to focus on changing little lifestyle habits — like moving more and eating less fat. Remember, over time, little bits add up.

If once and a while, you experience a few setbacks, that's okay. Everyone hits a slump now and then. Just remember, you can always recover by taking a quick refresher course — like walking a 45¢ bag of M&M's out to your local football field.

For those of you who read straight through this book in several hours without practicing such games as the *M&M Walk*, you can still flip back a few pages and participate in such exercises as the *Football-Field Walk* (pg. 81). Then you'll know how it really feels to walk off one M&M.

Best wishes for a great year of **Walking Off Weight**!

❖　　　　　❖　　　　　❖